A PICTORIAL MEMOIR

by SYLVIA ROTHENBERGER MILLER

Sylvia Rothenberger Miller

A PICTORIAL MEMOIR

by SYLVIA ROTHENBERGER MILLER

IN THE BEGINNING

NATURE—YES

PEOPLE—YES

ART—YES

THE LOWELL PRESS / KANSAS CITY

FIRST EDITION
Copyright 1980 by Sylvia Rothenberger Miller
L.C. 80-81146 ISBN 0-913504-57-2

This book has been printed in the United States of America on Warren's Flokote Enamel,
an acid-free paper with an expected 300-year library storage life as determined by the
Council of Library Resources of the American Library Association
by
The Lowell Press, Inc. / Kansas City, Missouri

Shown in this 120-page book are 141-full-color photographs
taken in 48 countries around the world.

In memory
of my parents
Kate W. Rothenberger and Harry B. Rothenberger
and to my husband
Arthur J. Miller

Author and photographer
Khajuraho, India

Photo courtesy of Betty Bricker

Prologue

A joy shared is rendered manifold; thus, I would share my joy with you.

I climbed rugged mountains, traversed limitless desert dunes, sailed oceans wide, descended into the depths of the earth, soared the heavens magnificent. Always I returned to a truism: human nature is everywhere unchanged and fundamentally unchangeable though indeed malleable and myriad in mode of life and living.

In the face of every child I found a gladsome, exultant "Yes!" to life, and because it was so, there is hope for the morrow.

Of little skill with brush or pen, I chose the enlarged vision of the camera's eye to preserve and to reflect that which my mind and my heart encompassed.

I sought truth and beauty, and I found them in nature, art, and the human condition.

Come share joy with me!

SYLVIA ROTHENBERGER MILLER

The
Handiwork
of
God

Southern Alps, New Zealand

Portage Glacier, Alaska

3

Nature—Yes

Seward Highway, Alaska

Te Anau Lake, New Zealand

Waterton Lakes National Park, Alberta, Canada

Sea coast, Tasmania, Australia

The Forest Primeval

Olympic National Park, Washington

God's

Promise

to

Man

Galapagos Islands

Victoria Falls, Rhodesia

Galapagos Islands

Glory
of the
Sea

Bora Bora, Society Islands

Galapagos Islands

11

Kith and Kinder

Kruger National Park, South Africa

Kruger National Park, South Africa

Kruger National Park, South Africa

The Beginning of the Divine Creation

New Caledonia

Sepik River, New Guinea

Sepik River, New Guinea

Malaita, Solomon Islands

Time
Stands
Still

Malaita, Solomon Islands

Goroka, New Guinea

Goroka, New Guinea

The Mudmen

Goroka, New Guinea

Goroka, New Guinea

Sepik River, New Guinea

Art—Yes

Sepik River, New Guinea

The Innocent and the Childlike

Malaita, Solomon Islands

Maroua, Cameroon

Maroua, Cameroon

People—Yes

Bamako, Mali

Bamako, Mali

The
Bottom Line

Bamako, Mali

Bamako, Mali

The
Human
Condition

Maroua, Cameroon

The Dignity
of
Labor

Maroua, Cameroon

Maroua, Cameroon

Addis Ababa, Ethiopia

Timbuktu, Mali

Maroua, Cameroon

L'élan vital!

Maroua, Cameroon

Kampala, Uganda

Kenya

Initiation Rites

South Africa

South Africa

Cairo, Egypt

Pyramids of Giza, Egypt

The Mind
and
the Hand
of Man

Sphinx, Egypt

Easter Island

Easter Island

The Silent Grandeur

Easter Island

Gobi Desert, Outer Mongolia

Gobi Desert, Outer Mongolia

Tears Love Laughter

Gobi Desert, Outer Mongolia

Gobi Desert, Outer Mongolia

Gobi Desert, Outer Mongolia

There is no God but God.

MUHAMMAD

Brunei, Borneo

Peshawar, Pakistan

Peshawar, Pakistan

Haute Cuisine

Landi Kotal at Khyber Pass, Pakistan

Lahore, Pakistan

The
Sound
of
Silence

Kabul, Afghanistan

Goreme, Turkey

Goreme, Turkey

Hamadan, Iran

Behold!

Let no evil come.

Katmandu, Nepal

Katmandu, Nepal

Katmandu, Nepal

My friend Papindar Pal Singh, Aurangabad Caves, India

Jaipur, India

New Delhi, India

Mandalay, Burma

The Truth:
I declare to you that
within the body you can
find the world, and the
origin of the world, and
the end of the world, and
the path—to all goals.

BUDDHA

Bangkok, Thailand

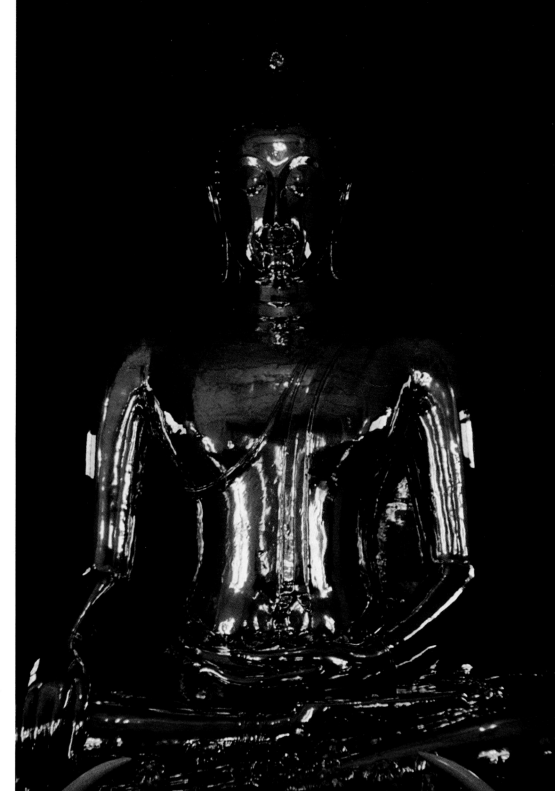

Chiang Mai, Thailand

The
Fundamental

The
Elemental

Chiang Mai, Thailand

The
Chief

New Caledonia

The
Subordinate

New Caledonia

Jogjakarta, Java, Indonesia

The
Laborers

Jogjakarta, Java, Indonesia (Batik)

Jogjakarta, Java, Indonesia

Music is the Pulse
of the Universe

Seoul, South Korea

Seoul, South Korea

Tana Island, New Hebrides

Nature,
Thy Name
is
Woman

Seoul, South Korea

Tokyo, Japan

Tokyo, Japan

Tokyo, Japan

The Joy of the Child

The Great Wall of China—
A Wonder of the World

Peking, China

Body

and

Mind

Peking, China

Kweilin, China

The Task

Kweilin, China

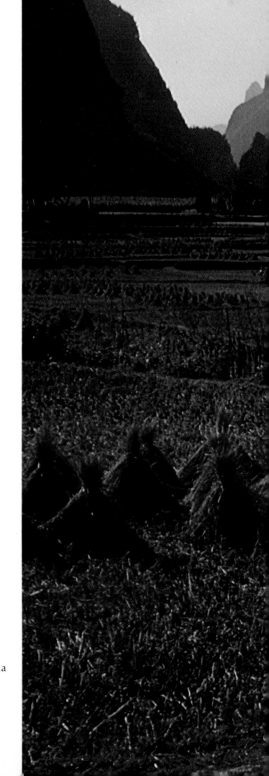

Kweilin, China

The Skill

Kweilin, China

Foshan City, China

The Tranquil Place

Kweilin, China

A Way of Life

Kweilin, China

Bora Bora, Society Islands

Life from the Sea

Fiji Island

Fiji Island

Fiji Island

The Cook

Fiji Island

New Caledonia

Moorea, Society Islands

The
Laughing
Hour

Moorea, Society Islands

Art—Yes

Maori carving, Rotorua, New Zealand

Aboriginal sculptures, Alice Springs, Australia

Aboriginal sculptures, Alice Springs, Australia

Behold
thy
Beauty

Anjouan Island, Comoros

Pago Pago, American Samoa

Dubrovnik, Yugoslavia

Time

Fatima, Portugal

The Timeless

Tananarive, Madagascar

Changsha, China

Santiago, Guatemala

Darjeeling, India

The Wonder
that is
the Child

Tananarive, Madagascar

The Lilt of Life

Lake Atitlan, Guatemala

Lake Atitlan, Guatemala

Antigua, Guatemala

Antigua, Guatemala

Hobart, Tasmania, Australia

The Lord is my shepherd;
I shall not want.

PSALMS 23

Norfolk, Tasmania, Australia

Damascus, Syria

The Street called Straight.

ACTS 9

Toledo, Spain

The Icon

Moscow, Russia

Innsbruck, Austria

Bacau, Romania

Rothenburg, Germany

The
Rothenberger
Origin

The Smile of Life

Romeo, Michigan

Ageless Beauty

Romeo, Michigan

Homeward Bound!

Boyne City, Michigan

Boyne City, Michigan

Romeo, Michigan

Home!

Romeo, Michigan

Davy

My mother and great-granddaughter Danya

My Mother
Had the privilege of choice been granted to me, I would not have chosen more wisely than she who was my own.

Romeo, Michigan

Epilogue

It is home again to the dearly familiar, and it is good that it be so.

From the sunrise of my world journey to its sunset, the grace of your presence has gladdened me, and I thank you for it, for indeed the sharing has made more manifold my joy.

Sylvia Rothenberger Miller